# WEATHER WISE

# WEATHER WISE

## LEONARD CRIMSON

# CONTENTS

1 Introduction to Meteorology — 1
2 Fundamentals of Weather Forecasting — 5
3 Key Elements of Weather — 9
4 Climate Patterns and Variability — 13
5 The Impact of Climate Change — 17
6 Weather Technology and Instruments — 21
7 Weather Safety and Preparedness — 25
8 Beyond the Forecast: Weather and Society — 29

Copyright © 2024 by Leonard Crimson
All rights reserved. No part of this book may be reproduced in any manner whatsoever without written permission except in the case of brief quotations embodied in critical articles and reviews.
First Printing, 2024

# CHAPTER 1

# Introduction to Meteorology

The study of weather is called meteorology. Scientists who study the weather are called meteorologists. The weather is the atmospheric conditions, along with short-term changes, of a certain place at a certain time. To help describe the weather, meteorologists use specific terminology. For example, air temperature is the amount of heat in the air. Precipitation is water, in solid or liquid form, that falls from the atmosphere. Humidity shows how much atmospheric moisture is present. Air pressure, or barometric pressure, is the amount of air pushing down on a certain area. Weather changes are produced by daily or weekly weather patterns.

The atmospheric conditions for longer periods of time is the area of climate studies. Over several decades, scientists examine temperature and precipitation patterns. Repeat weather patterns make up a climate. For example, if it is usually warm, dry, and sunny in a particular region, the climate of that region is warm, dry, and sunny. Studying weather and understanding how the atmosphere works are the main objectives of meteorology. The instruments meteorologists use today to predict and measure weather conditions modern technology has made it possible for meteorologists to forecast the weather with extraordinary accuracy. They can use satellites to study the development of weather features. They use computer models that make complex calculations. Through these forecasts, we can be warned and take protective actions for dangerous events such as hurricanes, tornadoes, and blizzards. As warnings are issued appropriately, far fewer injuries and deaths occur.

*Basic Concepts and Terminology*

As with any branch of the physical sciences, meteorology has its own concepts and terminology. Most of these are not difficult to understand, but it is necessary that the student understand them before he proceeds. For example, the atmosphere is the foundation of weather; consequently, in order to understand weather, we should start with this fundamental principle: The atmosphere, in a most general sense, is a warm gas whirling rapidly in the vicinity of the earth.

In studying daily weather conditions, the meteorologist is confronted with three classes of phenomena and must be conversant when discussing them. One of these classes of phenomena is known as the elements of the weather. It includes temperature, humidity, cloudiness, and so on. The second class of phenomena deals with weather conditions, such as fog, rain, thunderstorms, etc. The third class of phenomena is well-known climatic patterns, such as cold waves, heat waves, and so on.

But more important than what the meteorological elements are is the scale with which they are measured. Why is this? Climate patterns are relatively simple, but they can be directly affected by weather. For instance, a summer month in Texas could experience as many as two to four rainfall events or none at all due to boundary collisions that are determined by the activity in the atmosphere over the central/eastern United States. While the methods to analyze the small-scale are similar to those on larger scales, the obs (i.e., what meteorologists observe) and analysis are in much greater detail. Meteorologists have to fit all these pieces of the puzzle into a coherent picture of what will occur on the weather map over North America and adjacent seas.

*The Role of Meteorologists*

Meteorologists are scientists who study and interpret weather phenomena in the atmosphere. They have sensors and instruments to monitor and measure temperature, atmospheric pressure, humidity, and winds. They also study cloud formations to further understand approaching weather events. They study patterns in weather and analyze available data to make predictions about approaching fronts and their associated weather. Meteorologists also have a wealth of training in understanding how hurricanes, tornadoes, and other severe weather events form. They often work alongside computer scientists and engineers who help maintain weather equipment like radars and weather satellites. These people are called atmospheric or space scientists or engineers. With all their help, meteorologists combine computer modeling, knowledge of climate and weather patterns, and analysis to make forecasts accurate to a degree.

Computer models, which use complex mathematical equations that mimic the Earth's atmosphere, are used to predict the weather. However, these models are not always accurate and can produce wildly incorrect forecasts. If volcano emissions block sunlight and cool the Earth, for instance, a model may not predict drastic changes, although a drop in temperature would be occurring. A forecast's precision relies on the expertise, experience, and understanding used by the meteorologist who created it. Some basic guidelines that meteorologists consider in producing accurate weather predictions include: Air tends to move from high pressure to low pressure.

Weather systems in the US tend to generally move from west to east due to our air flow pattern called the jet stream. Cold fronts and areas of low pressure are associated with stormy, wet weather. Warm fronts tend to bring more mild and cloudy weather.

## CHAPTER 2

# Fundamentals of Weather Forecasting

Weather-wise: Understanding weather forecasts and climate patterns: Part 1

Overview of forecasts and forecasting Fundamentals of weather forecasting Weather forecast fundamentals Weather forecasting is all about predicting conditions of the atmosphere at a given location in the future. These predictions are made considering the current and past weather conditions, keeping in mind factors such as the speed and direction of winds, humidity, air pressure, and visibility. The process of trying to forecast the weather often begins with understanding what the weather is like now, or at a given time and place. These observations used in the forecast may range widely, from simple temperature measurements being taken with a thermometer to more complex measurements such as radar readings that are used in tracking thunderstorms.

How forecasts are done Forecasts are made by blending these measurements with knowledge developed about the behavior of the atmosphere over the years. The forecasts for the next few days commonly made by television and radio broadcasters use the statistics of weather observations, or weather data, from the past. Our Air Force

Weather Agency develops forecasts around the world using powerful computer models that paint a picture of the future by solving equations that describe the way the atmosphere behaves. With these complex computer models, meteorologists are able to look at forecast details over a select area down to a small scale, perhaps even just a few square miles. The observant pilot will notice that the Weather Officer may call on different equipment for local weather predictions. Weather conditions can be forecast locally using many kinds of equipment, from a log of temperature, wind speed, and sky condition observations, to the smallest nuclear powered, remote read-out, fully automatic electronic instrument. Weather predictions are made from a large number of measurements taken with weather balloons, radar, and satellite in several places around the earth. These data are blended together using one or more of the techniques that have been developed to help process the ever-increasing amounts of information. Among these computing systems is the implementation of a digital form of the model on a supercomputer. Requires a goodly number of processing cycles, but that's not so much of a limitation with the new super machines. The computer model forecasts the different kinds of weather and forecasts the weather several hours ahead, up to a week and a half ahead. Computer models of the weather science utilize a mathematical model, based on the physical properties of the earth and its atmosphere. The current condition at a number of locations in the earth's atmosphere are input into the computer, and the computational physics begins. The computer divides the atmosphere up into a three-dimensional grid and applies the equations for the physical laws governing the behavior of the atmosphere, equations that describe the change in pressure, temperature, wind, and so on, at each point in the grid during a given period. There are various models, designed for varying sophistication and complexity, used around the world. The accuracy of long-range weather forecasting continues to improve as the science of atmospheric forecasting continues to advance, fall in the range of 80% accuracy.

*Weather Observations and Data Collection*

Weather observations or monitoring form the basis of everything we know about weather and climate conditions. The sensor-based network used in automatic weather observation has one or more sensors monitoring the atmospheric conditions. Radio transmitters are often used to send measurements to a central data logger. More sophisticated versions use satellite or cellular technology to send data to where it can be used. One of the unique features of automatic weather stations (AWS) is that they can collect data about simultaneous weather patterns wherever they are situated and send them to a data center for storage and processing.

To make a reliable forecast, meteorologists need the right, good, accurate data that has been collected in as many places as possible. However, we do not have a weather station everywhere. For a continental landmass, the weather station network has to be sufficient to provide information about weather patterns at the surface. The information also needs to come from observation at different levels within the lowest levels of the atmosphere. The latest research has shown that, run through the cloud supercomputer at speeds of 6,000 trillion calculations a second, the model can provide a forecast accurate to 1 kilometer in around an hour. These much faster, high-resolution forecasts provide some very detailed information on how a storm might behave in the short-term. The more detailed the starting point, the more detailed and accurate the forecast out to seven days can be.

*Forecasting Techniques and Models*

There are several techniques and models in use by meteorologists to arrive at weather predictions. Some of the time-tested forecasting models and methods, which are in vogue, are as follows:

Empirical Prediction Models: Early weather predictions, say for 2 to 3 days, are carried out by using various empirical forms derived by using statistical analysis.

Characteristic Model Techniques: According to these models, the value of weather elements fluctuates around the mean values, and the bigger the fluctuation, the higher its importance.

Analog Technique: In this approach, previous weather maps at certain intervals of time are studied, and a pattern is induced for the concerned weather element of the present day. The pattern may be based on the wind direction, pressure distribution, shape of isobar, etc. This is, therefore, considered the most accurate technique.

Synoptic Techniques: The technique is based on identifying the origin, track, and pattern of movement of the cyclonic systems and anticyclones which bring stormy and clear weather respectively. Modern statistical and digital operations can help measure a real-time forecast more accurately and quickly, with the new prediction models which can determine not only the weather but also its effect on agriculture.

**CHAPTER 3**

# Key Elements of Weather

Day-to-day weather depends on the location and influence of high-pressure systems, areas of high pressure and usually fair weather, and low-pressure systems, areas of low pressure and stormy weather. High and low-pressure systems are caused by the movement of air masses across the United States and the wider world. Higher levels in the atmosphere can also affect weather conditions. Additionally, local processes, such as humidity and precipitation, as well as diurnal temperature variations, can influence weather in your area.

Pressure systems such as high and low-pressure systems directly influence weather conditions because they help establish the wind patterns in an area. Wind can move and transport air masses which, in turn, bring changes in air temperature and moisture content, and can shift the characteristics of the weather in an area. Understanding how pressure systems work and what happens when they interact can provide insight into predictions about upcoming weather. Temperature is also an important consideration. If you live in the desert, obviously precipitation is not going to play a large factor in the weather affecting your area and forecasts. Coastal areas may be influenced by water temperature, air masses of polar or tropical origin, and seasonal variations in their weather on a local scale.

*Temperature and Pressure Systems*

Temperature and pressure are used to divide Earth's atmosphere into layers, creating a marked distinction between the different air types in each. Temperature and pressure are what shape the movement and behavior of air masses or systems. Without them, the only influence on the atmosphere would be the rotation of Earth. Temperature is usually one of the first things people think of when they think of the atmosphere. Temperature is simply an expression of energy and direction of heat flow. It can change rapidly or slowly depending on the conditions. However, in any case, changes in temperature usually mean that the system is not stable. These changes also occur due to shifts of local conditions like solar radiation, topography, and surface properties and wildfires. As you can imagine, temperature is quite unstable and creates enormous variability in the atmosphere. Because temperatures vary so much around the planet, this creates differences in air densities and subsequently pressure.

At the surface, the pressure is created by the air column and the layer of air between us and the top of the atmosphere. The weight of the overlying air and its location will create differences and similarities of upward or downward motion and it can evolve over the time span of minutes to days. That means it forces the atmosphere to change pressure as heat and density change to form high pressure, low pressure, or some pressure in between. Even more, regions abound where the air columns are equal, and the pressure is steady. This is where a uniform temperature is present in the lower atmosphere. So, like temperature, pressure is a response to horizontal temperatures, with this being one of the main reasons we have weather patterns on our planet.

*Humidity and Precipitation*

As moisture content changes in the atmosphere, many different weather phenomena change. From the simple arrival of clouds to the complex evolution of thunderstorms, a deep understanding of humidity is critical in meteorology. Therefore, accurately determining moisture content and where the moisture will go is of critical importance in weather forecasting. Not only is humidity a short-term and long-term (climate) quantity of interest, but it is also a leading aspect of coupled oceanic-atmospheric circulation patterns which can affect seasonal precipitation patterns globally. In this subsection, we explain humidity and its quantification in regard to these issues. In the next subsections, we expand the topic of precipitation from a day-to-day analysis to seasonal forecasting as well as the relationships that exist between precipitation and atmospheric circulation.

From a synoptic (day-to-day) and short-term forecasting viewpoint, precipitation occurrence is often closely linked to the presence of synoptic-scale circulations. For example, the usual cloud patterns (e.g. lines of clouds associated with low-pressure troughs) are well-known surface weather patterns. They appear early during the development of frontal systems, usually at the warm front, and close to the center of the system. The physics of precipitation production is quite complex and depends upon the vertical distributions of temperature, humidity, and phase and size of hydrometeors present in cloud systems. Humid conditions, as we shall see below, are necessary but not sufficient to produce rain. However, for short-range forecasting, the amount of moisture in the sub-cloud layer can be used to verify short-term precipitation possibility in the warm air advection situations. We discuss this connection in later paragraphs.

## CHAPTER 4

# Climate Patterns and Variability

Over many centuries, meteorologists and scholars' cultural knowledge developed "folk knowledge" of the sky to read and forecast the weather. It's a local knowledge that visualizes present conditions instead of larger-scale contexts and does not need to consider influencing factors. Besides local surroundings, weather also fluctuates as an integral part of broader patterns and processes that exist within the components of the ocean and the atmosphere. Here we will discuss larger climate systems separate by their characteristics. Firstly, they are variable, and the relative timing, strength, or location varies from one event to another. El Niño is the warm phase of the El Niño-Southern Oscillation (ENSO) phenomenon in the central and eastern equatorial Pacific Ocean. La Niña is the cold phase of ENSO and is defined by cooler than typical sea surface temperatures. Diverse phenomena ranging from wildfires to flooding substantial rain effects occur in South America, while parts of Africa and Asia suffer from drought conditions.

The presentation so far might lead you to underestimate the relevance of large climate patterns by emphasizing ENSO as the most studied topic. But ENSO is not the solely large-scale climatic event, neither is it a global event. Within the ENSO basin, approximately five degrees north and south of the equator, ENSO is a critical component. However, all aspects do not appear to be as optimistic. Since ENSO swings around the equatorial rainfall, ENSO events can also contribute to ENSO "teleconnections" and influence weather patterns all over the globe. On the other hand, some large climate patterns and effects are truly global in nature; in other words, all land areas and oceans are affected. The most crucial one in the world is related to global circulation.

*Global Climate Systems*

The atmosphere and oceans are responsible for the continual climate adjustment of the planet. There are numerous temporal and spatial scales in play, producing various climate variability. This variability can be influenced by the following global climate systems: El Niño Southern Oscillation (ENSO), Arctic Oscillation (AO), Indian Ocean Dipole (IOD), North Atlantic Oscillation (NAO), Pacific North American Oscillation (PNA), and the Southern Oscillation (SO).

Global climate systems that have a significant influence on Canadian weather. Large-scale atmospheric patterns result from the dynamic processes occurring in the atmosphere, influenced by patterns of global-scale convection and the Earth's rotation. In the picture of the Earth, the 5 dynamic systems. The Earth's rotation results in a change in the meridional direction of the wind from pressure centre, known as the "winds aloft". This can be seen as a dextral (clockwise) rotation around the pressure centre in the Northern Hemisphere and a sinister (counter-clockwise) rotation in the Southern Hemisphere. The zonal wind system is in the same direction as the rotation of the Earth but contrasts with this as the jet stream winds travel from west to east, usually in the high latitudes of both hemispheres.

The meridional wind system, however, bends clockwise towards the pole in the Northern Hemisphere and bends towards the equator in the Southern Hemisphere. Atmospheric circulation is also markedly different with air of much cooler temperature and higher pressure moving away from the poles and warmer, low pressure air moving to them. The tropopause is the dividing line between the stratosphere and the ionosphere and is a boundary between the upper atmospheric and the lower atmosphere. In the stratosphere, temperature and wind direction of a constant decreasing and increasing nature are occasionally experienced, explaining the jet stream tendency to remain at the same level for lengthy periods of time.

*El Niño and La Niña Phenomena*

Another regularly happening climate pattern originating in the tropical Pacific is the El Niño/Southern Oscillation. At irregular intervals, these ocean reactions can influence a significant number of same climate designs that the Pacific Decadal Oscillation impacts, such as the area and power of hurricanes and the pace of El Niño. A standout forecasting errand is hurricane forecasting. An El Niño which is forecasted ahead of time can simplify forecast. It is foreseen that El Niño will be announced in an ideal manner. However, while forecasting El Niño and La Niña both, unfavourable activities have additionally been used; guidance has been less successful in recent years. One of the most dramatic and noteworthy climatic incidents is the El Niño. It happens at times, fluctuating from every 2 to 7 years. El Niño is connected with anomalous, or abnormal, climate phenomena, such as lowered rainy seasons or are sometimes more intense than regular.

These anomalous climate phenomena impact the international atmosphere, and that is the main cause why society is paying more attention to El Niño; in one way or another, almost all weather models include the probable phenomena of El Niño. La Niña is the twin-sister of El Niño. It is the case where the normal Pacific trade winds go entirely in the opposite direction of El Niño. Meteorologists are continually estimating and forecasting future climate, usually for a period of several days to a week. La Niña is the analogous situation of El Niño, it is characterized by a cooling of the ocean and significant weather pattern variations. El Niño and La Niña have global impacts on the weather. La Niña usually opposes the "normal" El Niño effects; for example, in areas where El Niño is given high rainfall, then La Niña causes a drought. The opposite situation is true moreover.

## CHAPTER 5

# The Impact of Climate Change

There is agreement among scientists that average global temperatures are rising as a result of human activities, primarily the burning of fossil fuels and deforestation. An increase of just 1 to 2 degrees in global temperatures may seem negligible, but consider that a difference of only 2.5 degrees separates our planet's average temperature during an ice age from the planet's average temperature today. As average global temperature increases, so too does the frequency and severity of dangerous weather phenomena, including hurricanes, tornadoes, heat waves, wildfires, floods, and droughts. Climate change also has the potential to exacerbate air and water pollution and contribute to an array of health problems, from heat stroke to respiratory distress to the proliferation of infectious diseases. Importantly, though global temperatures are rising, the relationship between climate and weather is a dynamic and complex one. Climate change will not manifest itself uniformly, and even in the areas where change does occur, the nature of that change may vary from year to year.

Our understanding of climate change has improved dramatically in the past century. Satellite measurements have allowed scientists to track large-scale environmental variables, such as atmospheric temperature, greenhouse gas concentration, sea level, and glacial mass. With their help, it has become clear that something has changed on a fundamental level. The earth's climate, and the many smaller systems that make up the complex interactions of our atmosphere, hydrosphere, lithosphere, and biosphere, are no longer operating according to the principles that guided them throughout known human history. The planet on which we once relied for a stable if capricious climate is now approaching environmental chaos. Notice that we say climate, not weather. Climate—rather than specific weather phenomena—is what is changing. The increased frequency of extreme weather events has been linked to climate change, but the time and place of individual occurrences still depends on the interaction of complex weather processes. Climate change has not created new systems so much as it has thrown existing mechanisms into disarray.

*Causes and Drivers of Climate Change*

The climate has changed across the history of the Earth as a result of natural factors. These natural factors are still the fundamental drivers of climate change at present and in the future. These factors include plate movements, volcanic eruptions, and variations in the energy generated by the Sun.

There are several factors that can affect the Earth's temperature at different timescales. One of the most important factors known to affect the Earth's temperature on very long timescales (greater than 10,000 years) is plate tectonics. However, the human impact on this factor is negligible. Volcanic eruptions in the mid- to long term have been recognized as one of the main drivers of climate change over the last 600 million years (the last six major glaciations). Volcanoes emit a mixture of gases and particles. Some of the gases are greenhouse gases and trap heat, therefore they warm the Earth. Volcanoes also emit sulfate aerosols, which reflect the Sun's rays and create a natural sunshade. Consequently, they have a cooling effect. The rate of solar output and changes in the way solar energy is distributed between the poles and the equator are additional factors that may have affected the climate. In the last 400 years, measurements of sunspot cycles show that the Sun's energy levels have stayed the same or have increased slightly, but this factor cannot explain all of the recent warming. After a volcanic eruption, erupted particles are removed from the atmosphere within 2 to 4 years. In contrast, $CO_2$ remains in the atmosphere for many years. The increased concentration of this gas in the atmosphere means that its warming effect accumulates over the long term. In summary, natural factors, particularly those resulting from volcanic emissions, play a major role in changing the climate over billions of years. However, human activities have and will alter the climate by emitting gases and particles, impacting the climate at regional, continental, and global levels.

*Implications for Weather Patterns*
Implications for weather patterns over time
The increasing incidence of extreme weather events - including more frequent heat waves, heavy precipitation, floods, and droughts - has prompted many to ask about possible implications of a changing climate. These events are the result of what Lotus Baker, then of the Committee for a Constructive Tomorrow, described in September as "the enormous and still unpredictable solar climate regulators acting as dampers on the delicate balance of uneven energy flows."

Newer scientific studies also point to dramatic changes in the patterns of wind currents and ocean temperatures as well as large-scale cloud formation resulting from rapidly melting Arctic sea ice. The loss of the reflective ice becomes what the State of Fear author calls "a self-smoking gun" as dark water absorbs more energy while emitting less of it than ice does. Sometimes, rapid formation of new sea ice - the formation process emits a lot of energy - can even heat the atmosphere straight away instead of cooling it, as fancy climate models had foreseen. Such events will increasingly affect weather patterns and temperature (and storm) predictions.

Moreover, both the hotter weather trends and the extreme events can drive the expansion of subtropical desert weather patterns. Baker explained that this is because the rising warm, moist air easily clouds over the subtropical oceans, where the tropics end, forming clouds with more moisture than can be rained out and hence shading the ground by reflecting away the sunshine. With more energy (temperatures) around to lift the air, there is a rise in what is called the lifting condensation level so that air takes longer to cool down to the recovery of the environment, thus becoming ripe with moisture - the building blocks of storms, hurricanes, and typhoons. It is a logical consequence.

## CHAPTER 6

# Weather Technology and Instruments

Weather radar is an atmospheric sounding tool that transmits microwaves through the sky. Some of the energy from the radar beam is reflected by water droplets, and this reflection makes a pattern on the screen. Areas containing relatively large amounts of water droplets are good indications of rain, hail, or snow. One of the most common uses for weather radar is to determine the location and strength of rain and snow. In the past few years, the National Weather Service has been installing a network of Doppler radars to help track thunderstorms, tornadoes, and falling rain and snow. A weather satellite is a type of satellite that is primarily used to monitor the weather and climate of Earth.

Weather satellites can be polar orbiting, covering the entire Earth asynchronously, or geostationary, hovering over the same spot on the equator. Moisture, temperature, and wind measurements taken from weather balloons above the surface of the Earth are routed together to provide a speed profile, a temperature profile, and a wind profile. This information is used to find patterns and relationships between temperature, wind, humidity, and air pressure, giving meteorologists a better understanding of existing weather and the factors responsible for weather changes. Automated weather stations make efficient use of instruments to measure many of the weather variables that scientists need to understand weather and climate. Many stations are also capable of sending their observations directly to a central collection facility, providing up-to-date information for meteorologists to use in forecasting. Balloons equipped with weather instruments carry these tools to nearly twice the height of airplane traffic. The instrument set at the end, called the radiosonde, collects temperature, humidity, pressure, and position information.

*Radar and Satellite Imaging*

Radar and satellite imaging help meteorologists see weather happening and take the guesswork out of some forecasting. Radar detects precipitation, clouds, and ice in the atmosphere. It emits weak microwave energy which bounces off matter in the atmosphere and returns a signal that is processed to create images of clouds and precipitation. The National Weather Service, including WICC at Valley City, KX at Pembina, BIS at Bismarck, and FGF at Grand Forks, operate Doppler radar. Instead of seeing stationary objects and a horizontal scan of the atmosphere, the radar can detect the direction of a moving object in the atmosphere such as rain, snow, hail, and even dust. A computer at a local radar site also uses radar data to determine where it is raining heaviest and the most likely place for severe weather.

The National Oceanic and Atmospheric Administration (NOAA) uses Geostationary Operational Environmental Satellite (GOES) satellites to spot developments which could affect national weather. National Weather Service forecasters use the imagery from computers in their offices. GOES satellites are like weather buoys in space. They do a great job of spotting large-scale storms of different frequencies as well as hurricanes. They generally stay in a stationary orbit 22,300 miles above the Earth and have to be replaced about every five to seven years to ensure their operation. The satellites use weather instruments such as imaging and temperature sensors that take detailed images of cloud patterns, sea surface temperature measurements, amount of radiant energy, and soundings of the atmosphere. The temperature sensor measures land and sea temperatures as well as cloud top temperatures. In reviewing this information, forecasters will then be able to see weather moves across the country and they can predict future weather conditions based on climate patterns.

*Weather Stations and Balloons*

Weather stations around the world provide observations, which are processed by computers to produce present conditions such as temperature, pressure, humidity, rain or snowfall, and visibility. These observations feed models, providing short-term forecasts of weather and enabling meteorologists to give warnings for storms and other forecast products.

Special weather balloons carry a variety of instruments and are released worldwide at least twice a day, usually at the same Coordinated Universal Time (UTC), which is similar to Greenwich Mean Time. The balloons are made of latex, rise up to 25 kilometers (15 miles), and burst. As they ascend through the atmosphere, they gather temperature, pressure, and humidity data that are transmitted to the ground stations in real time by a system of radiosondes.

The radiosondes gather information that is converted into relative humidity and dew point, information that is invaluable in the accurate forecasting of severe weather and flash floods. Similarly, the information gathered by all the weather balloons helps to populate models that produce medium-range forecasts that, thanks to powerful computers, go on up to sixteen days. Median-range outlooks that cover week 2 and week 3 are developed based on the experimental Subseasonal Experiment Model Ensemble (SEMEREEK) and the National Multi-Model Ensemble (NMME). And just as important, data collected from weather balloons, in addition to satellite-based data and on-the-ground observations made at weather stations, contribute to a variety of research projects that are part of the nation's several Earth observation programs. National agencies and universities fly balloons, as do the European Centre for Medium-Range Weather Forecasts (ECMWF) and many agencies in Asia, as well as the World Meteorological Society (WMO).

## CHAPTER 7

# Weather Safety and Preparedness

Thunderstorms, lightning, heat, tornadoes, and floods are some of the hazards that accompany weather. Understanding when and where these events will occur, including the potential impacts, provides essential information that supports response activities. The National Weather Service is the primary source for severe weather warnings, products, and guidance. Detailed emergency planning should be implemented for any dangerous events that threaten your area.

The safety of you and your family is your primary concern. In many instances, you will have the time needed to seek appropriate shelter. However, a rapidly developing event, such as a tornado, will require an immediate response. When severe weather threatens your area, monitor the forecasts and possible threatened areas closely. Severe weather statements will often be updated frequently. As the weather situation develops, listen to NOAA Weather Radio or TV for updates on any watches and warnings that are issued for your area. Make sure to have a family emergency plan that covers all types of local hazards. A weather safety plan should include where to shelter in the event of a tornado or severe storm. Make sure all members of your family are familiar with the plan and have gone through tornado/evacuation drills and have basic weather safety knowledge. For additional information, visit Ready.gov, which is designed to help families prepare for emergencies.

It is state emergency managers and local officials who are charged with managing the overall needs of the public during a weather disaster and those responsible for preventing or reducing losses from hazards. Having a plan in place will minimize disruption to your family, school, or business. Know the safe areas in your own home, workplace, or school and the trusted buildings in which to take refuge. Knowing the basics will help you respond quickly to stay safe during actual emergencies. Whether it is a hazardous materials spill, an extreme winter storm, a tornado, a severe thunderstorm, or a large spreading wildland fire, having a safety plan in place can prevent injury and save lives.

*Understanding Severe Weather Warnings*

After all the painstaking effort taken to predict the weather, meteorological agencies often issue severe weather warnings to the public to alert them to the potential dangers. Severe weather warnings typically deal with thunderstorms, floods, wind damage, heavy rainfall, bombogenesis, typhoons, and sediment or ash eruptions. Civil defense, coastguard, and other emergency services use these warnings to help prepare for the impending event. There is a growing desire from both the forecast public and users such as electricity companies, transport authorities, and local government to receive even more information on the impacts that weather may bring in order to plan more effectively. Both regional forecasters and national agencies issue severe weather warnings.

The information contained in a severe weather warning is divided into three parts: 1. announcement 2. situation where and how the weather is likely to impact on you 3. prognosis the likely outcome of the event. Additional information may be added in remarks where forecasters can include their expert interpretation and information not already covered in the three parts. A severe weather warning is not just issued because of forecast weather but also if actual weather is likely to lead to disaster situations. The warning continues until the forecast weather changes, the event has occurred, or the risk has passed.

*Emergency Planning and Response*
Most visits to the local police department, fire department, or emergency management office are for things like reports, clearances, equipment testing, budget meetings, and community events.

Emergency Management Director Larry Smith says the Community Emergency Response Team class is the beginning of trying to change that. These are the people who answered the call. The class meets for the fourth of six weeks, learning basic disaster response skills, such as fire safety, light search and rescue, team organization, and disaster medical operations. The ultimate goal of the class is community preparedness. During an initial disaster, such as the storm that hit parts of Dauphin County last Thursday, local fire crews, police, public works employees, and the Dauphin County Emergency Management Agency work together for an effective, sometimes life-threatening response.

The response went well, Smith said, especially in light of the fact that when the storm hit, 97 percent of those officials were in Hershey dealing with a seminar at the Penn State Hershey Medical Center. "You really don't have enough time to think," said Hummelstown Fire Chief Tim Llewellyn, who spent several hours coordinating public safety responders Thursday.

CHAPTER 8

# Beyond the Forecast: Weather and Society

Some of the major aspects of societies that are affected by, or otherwise proactive in the realm of weather, relate to agriculture and transportation. Weather patterns also influence conflict and public health. We discuss three of these briefly below.

Weather and Agriculture Agriculture is widely recognized as being weather-sensitive. In Canada, lower levels of precipitation during anomalous dry patterns of a trio of months between April and September will reduce the wheat yield unless irrigation equipment is employed. This is one way agriculture is an illustration of an integral resource sector that must adapt. Staple crops are sowed every year by more than 51,000 farmers with 19 million acres of land across Western Canada. With record ice trends in travel, transportation infrastructures have had to adapt. The giant pendant 16-foot-diameter bears the brunt of 1200 vcfs currently headed for the Pattullo Bridge in Surrey, increasing congestion on the Port Mann Bridge.

Weather and Inland Waterway Transportation One of the major problems with waterway transportation is variability – rain patterns can change and raise streamflows out of safe boating range. If we see a tipping point, mitigation strategies can be used to reduce the impacts of these disasters if they are found to be directly caused by certain weather patterns. Public health departments also frequently work to communicate ways in which the public can adapt to health risks, such as strategies for keeping cool or keeping informed about a particular epidemic. If communities ignore mandated emergency evacuations in the face of incoming hurricanes, then the analysis can delve into why.

*Weather's Influence on Agriculture*

It is no secret that weather is one of the most important factors for farmers. Weather determines when most things are done on the farm, and in some cases, it can be a life or death situation. To plant, it is necessary for the weather to be warm enough. Then, it is necessary to have adequate humidity and rain for the crops to grow. Next, the crops need sunny days, so the plants can make the energy they need to grow. Then, it needs to stop raining, so the crops can be gathered and machinery can be used again in the field without making mud. After the crops are gathered, the cool weather is needed again so the grain can be stored until it can be sold.

Weather conditions determine the window of time in which farmers must complete field work and what type of equipment must be used to do it. Farmers have a lot of equipment in the barn, such as tractors, combines, and disks. But which piece of equipment farmers use at a certain time of year is determined by the weather outside. The weather also influences the clothes that people wear. Farmers look at the weather forecast to help them decide when is the best time to do something. Many farmers also use something called a "rain gauge" to measure the amount of rain that has fallen. It is this combination of needing to get things done and the weather's influence that is why it is important to study agriculture students to understand how these two interrelate.

*Weather's Impact on Transportation*

Weather has a central role in the functioning of transportation systems. It has enormous day-to-day importance, directly affecting travel, safety, and ultimately, how the world works. Climate is an essential long-term consideration, dictating how transportation systems are designed and planned. Weather patterns have always influenced travel. But the shifting climate patterns, particularly in the last 30 years, have exacerbated the weather's disruptive impact. From a long-term perspective, we are seeing increased frequency and severity of heavy rain events, as well as changes to freeze/thaw cycles, snow coverage, and fire risk.

Transportation is particularly impacted by adverse weather. For railway systems, lightning-caused fires or flash floods are often less significant disruptions than either a series of high-heat running rail days or deep cold spells. As such, the impacts of changes in conditions can cause major problems, from slow orders to the need for enhanced track maintenance. Airplane turbulence and airport operation decisions are heavily influenced by weather. Again, while the impacts of changing weather are often less severe than the impacts from surface effects, because fewer travelers are flying during these conditions, the consequences of a decision error can be life-threatening. Policymakers, stakeholders, and engineers need to predict these impacts to make cost-efficient systems, and as such are interested in predictions of various time spans, from 24-hour operational forecasts to seven-day advance notices, to seasonal and longer-time scale climate monitoring. Meteorologists can supply this information. More time information is not always better, and long-term climate patterns can improve predictions of severe events. Nonetheless, people cognitively understand varying lengths of time scales differently. Long-term patterns are useful for uncovering useful impacts and improving the form and color of the basic forecast.

www.ingramcontent.com/pod-product-compliance
Lightning Source LLC
LaVergne TN
LVHW092102060526
838201LV00047B/1523